CHERUBS

CHERUBS

A JOYOUS CELEBRATION

COURAGE BOOKS

AN IMPRINT OF RUNNING PRESS
PHILADELPHIA • LONDON

Printed in China

9   8   7   6   5   4   3   2   1
Digit on the right indicates the number of this printing

Library of Congress Cataloging-in-Publication Number 98-70168

ISBN 0-7624-0344-6

Design by Frances J. Soo Ping Chow
Introduction by Sonya Beard
Edited by Gena M. Pearson
Pictures researched by Susan Oyama

Published by Courage Books, an imprint of
Running Press Book Publishers
125 South Twenty-second Street
Philadelphia, Pennsylvania 19103-4399

CONTENTS

INTRODUCTION

Perhaps the most beautiful thing about cherubs is our belief in them. Witnesses of cherub sightings speak of the warmth they bestow, their illuminous glow, and the love that radiates from these childlike angels. Indeed, history seems to confirm their existence. Throughout the ages, they have come to represent that eternal part of human nature that seeks relief from the cynicism of day-to-day life. Cherubs have an elemental appeal. They satisfy our thirst for ideal love. The contradiction between their infantile state and their natural wisdom enchants us. Their innocent notions and untarnished view captivate what is virtuous in us.

To understand the significance of cherubs, we must go beyond the physical, or even the traditional mythological labels. They surpass the natural and dwell within the supernatural realm. To some, they are a conscience and a guide. Others have said they have experienced their wonder through a beam of light or a simple touch. And some even claim to have seen them in animals.

Winged naked infants, intercessors between heaven and earth, Cupid, heavenly spirits, *putti*, celestial beings—whatever cherubs are called by different cultures and religions—they fascinate us. They have flown from history into mainstream pop culture and right into our hearts. They represent all that is good in the world.

In the past, cherubs were described as part of the angelic hierarchy. They were next in order behind the *seraphim*, or six-winged angles. Originally, the word *cherub* referred to a winged sphinx-like figure with the head of a human and the body of an animal. They were placed in the doorways of churches and palaces to serve as divine intercessors and guardians. In many religions, they still signify power and majesty. It is, however, more fantastical to color reality with our own visions of how illustrious cherubs are—or how they *could* be.

For centuries, poets, artists, writers, and musicians the world over have sought to capture these wonderful creatures in image, words, and song. Collected here are some of the finest examples of those efforts—a reminder of the warmth of celestial love, the joy of innocence, and the beauty and grace of the human imagination.

CREATURES OF LIGHT

IF we saw an angel clearly, we should die of pleasure.

BRIGETT OF SWEDEN (1303–1373)
SWEDISH NOBLEWOMAN, MYSTIC, AND FOUNDER OF BRIDGETTINE NUNS

The most beautiful and most profound emotion

we can experience is the sensation of the mystical.

ALBERT EINSTEIN (1879–1955)
GERMAN BORN AMERICAN PHYSICIST

There are two worlds; the world that we can measure with line and rule,

and the world that we feel with our hearts and imagination.

LEIGH HUNT (1784–1859)
ENGLISH WRITER

BUT EVERYWHERE THERE IS . . . A SENSE OF SOMETHING TRANSCENDING

THE EXPECTED OR NATURAL, A SENSE OF THE EXTRAORDINARY, MYSTERIOUS, OR SUPERNATURAL.

Robert H. Lowie (1883–1957)
American anthropologist

According to those who believe in them, angels can take an almost infinite variety of forms;

an unseen force, a bright light, an animal, a touch, a mysterious stranger.

DAWN RAFFEL
AMERICAN WRITER

Rose looked up. To her amazement there stood an angel.

She wasn't any taller than Rose herself, with blond hair and

a halo that was tilted just a little bit. Everything about her

had a glow, unlike anything Rose had ever seen.

DEBBY BOONE (B. 1956)
AMERICAN WRITER

17

. . . ANGELS HAVE GARMENTS WHICH GLITTER AS WITH FLAME,

AND SOME ARE RESPLENDENT AS WITH LIGHT. . . .

A. S. Byatt
American writer

. . . cherubim were often described as blue or wearing blue, as befits the possessors and bestowers of wisdom: They pour forth wisdom in floods.

SOPHY BURNHAM
AMERICAN WRITER

WHAT STOOD OUT THE MOST FOR ME WAS THE WARM LIGHT
THAT RADIATED FROM HIM. I'VE NEVER SEEN HIM AGAIN,
BUT WHENEVER I GET A WARM FEELING—I KNOW HE'S NEARBY.

Ingrid Herrera (b. 1966)
Guatemalan wife and mother

21

LIKE LIVING FLAME THEIR FACES

SEEMED TO GLOW, THEIR WINGS WERE GOLD.

AND ALL THEIR BODIES SHONE

MORE DAZZLING WHITE THAN ANY EARTHLY SHOW.

Dante Alighieri (1265–1321)
Italian poet

[ANGELS ARE] Elemental Spirits of the universe whose duration and movement are outside the limitations of tidy time and whose principal activities are knowing and willing; bearers of Archaic knowledge and wisdom.

MARY DALY
AMERICAN WRITER AND SCHOLAR

22

ANGELS ARE SPIRITS IMMATERIAL AND INTELLECTUAL, THE GLORIOUS INHABITANTS OF THOSE SACRED PLACES WHERE THERE IS NOTHING BUT LIGHT AND IMMORTALITY.

Richard Hooker (1554–1600)
English theologian

. . . creatures of a spiritual nature, gifted with

intellect and free will, superior to man.

POPE JOHN PAUL II (B. 1920)
ROMAN CATHOLIC CLERIC

25

We not only live among men, but there are airy hosts, blessed spectators sympathetic lookers-on that see and know and appreciate our thoughts and feelings and acts.

Henry Ward Beecher (1813–1887)
American cleric and newspaper editor

ANGELS

SPEAK TO US THROUGH OUR THOUGHTS. . . .

Terri Lynn Taylor
American writer

. . . ANGELS PULL BACK THE CURTAIN,

HOWEVER BRIEFLY, ON THE REALM OF THE SPIRITS.

Nancy Gibbs
American writer

Angels exist through the eyes of faith, and faith is perception.

Only if you can perceive it can you experience it.

REVEREND JOHN WESTERHOFF
AMERICAN THEOLOGIAN

And even if they do not exist, is not the very thought of them

an active warrant of their reality as causes? For are not thoughts causes?

FREDERICK TURNER (B. 1943)
ENGLISH WRITER

ANGELS ARE PURE THOUGHTS FROM GOD,

WINGED WITH TRUTH AND LOVE. . . .

Mary Baker Eddy (1821–1910)
American theologian

Their appearances may be rare,
but angels are no endangered species.

They move and work still.

TIMOTHY JONES (B. 1948)
AMERICAN WRITER

MILLIONS OF SPIRITUAL CREATURES WALK THE EARTH

UNSEEN, BOTH WHEN WE SLEEP AND WHEN WE WAKE.

John Milton (1608–1674)
English poet

Make yourself familiar with the angels, and behold them frequently

in spirit; for without being seen, they are present with you.

SAINT FRANCIS DE SALES (1567–1622)
FRENCH CLERIC AND WRITER

THAT there are angels and spirits

good and bad . . . is so clear. . . . That

no believer, unless he be first of all spoiled

by philosophy and vain deceit, can possi-

bly entertain a doubt of it.

RICHARD HURD (1720–1808)
ENGLISH CLERIC

It is not known precisely where angels dwell—whether in the air, the void, or the planets. It has not been God's pleasure that we should be informed of their abode.

VOLTAIRE (1694–1778)
FRENCH WRITER

ANGELS ARE metaphors. They carry us from one realm to another. They are "tongues in trees, books in the running brooks, sermons in the stones, and good in every thing."

F. FORRESTER CHURCH (B. 1948)
AMERICAN WRITER

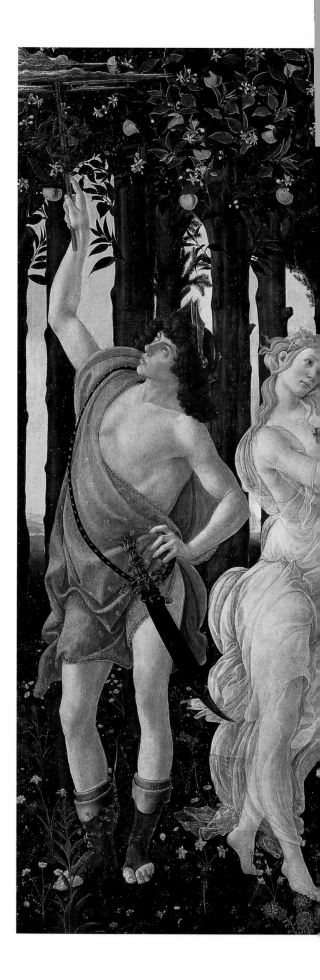

THE ANGELS KEEP THEIR ANCIENT PLACES;

TURN BUT A STONE, AND START A WING!

'TIS YE, 'TIS YOUR ESTRANGED FACES,

THAT MISS THE MANY-SPENDOURED THING.

Francis Thompson (1859–1907)
English poet

Angels work with our souls, in conjunction with the Universal Mind, to help us raise our sights and spirits by reminding us of the truth, beauty, and goodness that exist within everything.

ALMA DANIEL, TIMOTHY WYLIE, AND ANDREW RAMER
AMERICAN WRITERS

So all we know of what they do above is that

they are happy, and that they love.

EDMUND WALLER (1606–1687)
ENGLISH POET

CREATURES OF LOVE

To love for the sake of being loved is human, but to love for the sake of loving is angelic.

ALPHONSE DE LAMARTINE (1790–1869)
FRENCH POET

In the time when herbs and flowers,

spring out of melting powers,

Teach the earth that heat and rain

do make Cupid live again.

FULKE GREVILLE (1554–1628)
ENGLISH POET

IF THERE IS ANYTHING THAT KEEPS THE

MIND OPEN TO ANGEL VISITS, AND REPELS THE

MINISTRY OF EVIL, IT IS PURE HUMAN LOVE.

Nathaniel Parker Willis (1806–1867)
American editor and writer

Angels are the simplest things to connect with. You'll find them in any place of innocence. And if you realize that everything is innocent, you realize the universe is safe. So wherever love is, they are. So they must be everywhere.

KATHERINE SCORZO
AMERICAN ARTIST

I believe that in the angelic realm,
　　　　　　　　there is no limitation.
There is all love.

CHUCK ALTEN
AMERICAN ENGINEER

HE WHO DEFENDS WITH LOVE WILL BE SECURE;

HEAVEN WILL SAVE HIM AND PROTECT HIM WITH LOVE.

Lao-tzu (6th century B.C.)
Chinese philosopher

Love rules the hour, the camp, the grove,

And man below and saints above:

For love is heaven and heaven is love.

Sir Walter Scott (1771–1832)
Scottish poet and writer

We are each of us angels with only one wing.

And we can only fly by embracing each other.

LUCIANO DE CRESCENZO (B. 1928)
ITALIAN WRITER

When the one man loves the one woman and the one woman loves the one man,

the very angels leave heaven and come and sit in that house and sing for joy.

ATTRIBUTED TO BRAHMA, THE HINDU GOD OF CREATION

Heaven is large, and affords space for all modes of love and fortitude.

RALPH WALDO EMERSON (1803–1882)
AMERICAN ESSAYIST AND POET

LOVE POSSESSES SEVEN HUNDRED WINGS, AND EACH ONE

EXTENDS FROM THE HIGHEST HEAVEN TO THE LOWEST EARTH.

Rumi (1207–1273)
Persian poet

Oh, there is nothing holier, in this life of ours,

than the first consciousness of love—the first fluttering of its silken wings.

HENRY WADSWORTH LONGFELLOW (1807–1882)
AMERICAN POET

LOVE TO FAULTS IS ALWAYS BLIND,

ALWAYS IS TO JOY INCLIN'D

LAWLESS, WING'D, AND UNCOFIN'D.

AND BREAKS ALL CHAINS FROM EVERY MIND.

William Blake (1757–1827)
English artist, poet, and mystic

Love is sure to be something less than human

if it is not something more.

COVENTRY K. D. PATMORE (1823–1896)
ENGLISH POET

Of all earthly music, that which reaches farthest into

heaven is the beating of a truly loving heart.

HENRY WARD BEECHER (1813–1887)
AMERICAN CLERIC

Tell me, dearest, what is love?

'Tis a lightning from Above;

'Tis an arrow, 'tis a fire,

'Tis a boy they call Desire. . . .

John Fletcher (1579–1652)
English writer

OF MAGIC SO POTENT OVER SUN AND STAR IS LOVE.

William Wadsworth (1770–1850)
English poet

There is music even in the beauty, and the silent note which Cupid strikes,

far sweeter than the sound of an instrument.

THOMAS BROWNE (1605–1682)
ENGLISH PHYSICIAN AND WRITER

73

Love looks not with the eyes, but with the mind,

and therefore is winged Cupid painted blind.

William Shakespeare (1564–1616)
English playwright and poet

BEACONS OF HOPE

THE GUARDIAN ANGELS OF LIFE SOMETIMES FLY SO HIGH

AS TO BE BEYOND OUR SIGHT, BUT THEY ARE ALWAYS LOOKING DOWN UPON US.

Jean Paul Richter (1765–1825)
German writer

...they are given to us as guardians.

SAINT AMBROSE (339–397)
ROMAN CLERIC

...[they are] beings who will take care of us....

ANDREW M. GREELEY (B. 1928)
AMERICAN CLERIC AND WRITER

They for us fight, they watch,

and duly ward,

And their bright squadrons round

about us plant:

And all for love, and nothing

for reward.

※

Edmund Spenser (1553–1599)

English poet

. . . such loyal companions guide her to the center,

of the wind,

to the place where the ancestors,

the stars, reside.

SANDRA BENÍTEZ (B. 1941)
AMERICAN WRITER

85

Angels have a way of lifting us and giving us hope.

Joan Webster Anderson
American writer

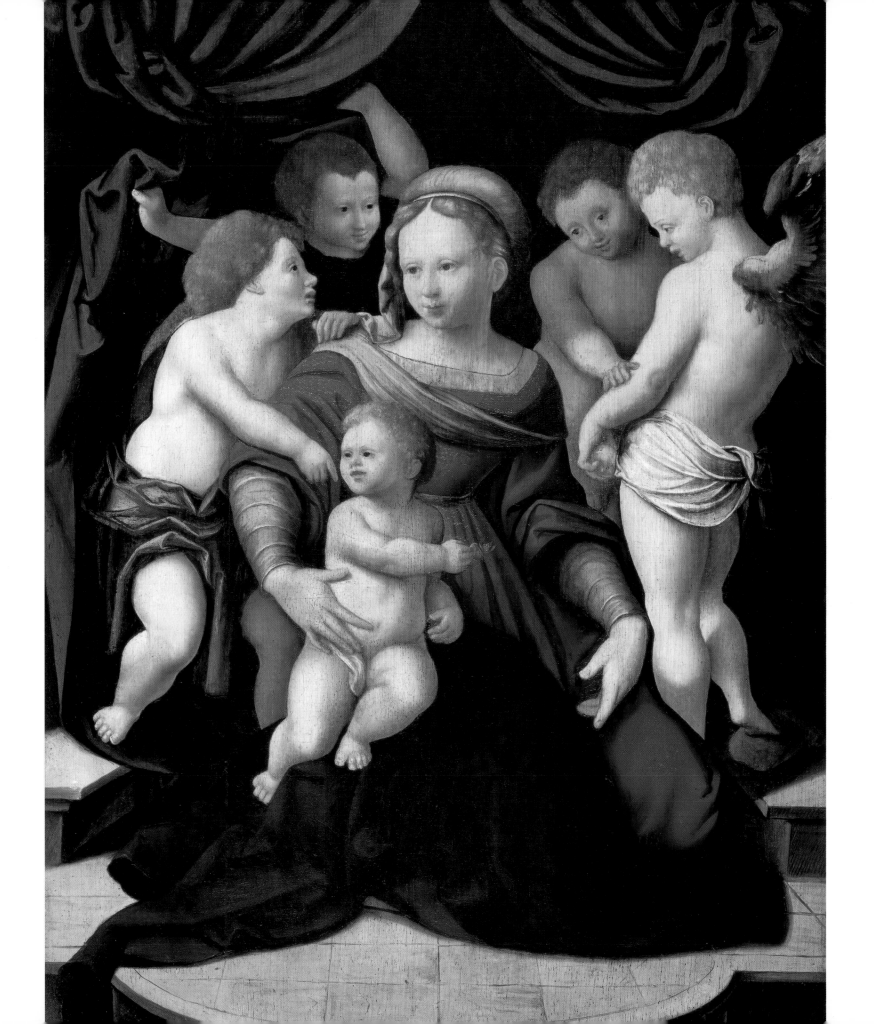

As the world gets scarier, as we get more concerned about violence,

we gravitate toward things that are comforting and make us feel safe.

NANCY CUSHMAN
AMERICAN ENTREPRENEUR

PEOPLE ARE HUNGRY FOR HOPE . . . ANGELS MAKE US KNOW

WE ARE LOVED. . . . THESE WONDERFUL BEINGS ARE PROTECTING US.

Sophy Burnham
American writer

Joy

is made of starlight, eternally young, inventive and high-spirited.

She is the guardian cherub, the angel of children. She is joyful.

DANA REYNOLDS
AMERICAN WRITER

Angels are guardians of people and all

physical things. For this reason, angels

and cherubs have been found for cen-

turies in the home.

GLADYS MACK
AMERICAN ART HISTORIAN

Every visible thing in this world is

put in the charge of an angel.

SAINT AUGUSTINE (354–430)
ROMAN PHILOSOPHER

We are never so lost
that our angels cannot find us.

STEPHANIE POWERS (B. 1942)
AMERICAN ACTRESS AND ACTIVIST

...ITAS · TVA · DEI · GENITRIX · VIRGO

ANGELIC ENCOUNTER LEAVES US CHANGED FOR THE BETTER. . . .

Eileen Elias Freeman
American writer

They may appear as other humans, as glorious flashes

of light, as a soft and unseen touch or as that 'still small voice'

that often speaks to us in times of crisis.

Bernard Ward
American writer

Cherubs came to reflect what was foremost on the American mind.

Be it war or peace, prosperity or depression,

they served as a chronicle of history, as well as a beacon of hope.

STEVEN C. PETTINGA
AMERICAN JOURNALIST

LIGHTSOME SPIRITS

How

sweetly did they float upon the wings

Of silence through the empty-vaulted night,

At every fall smoothing the raven down

Of darkness 'til it smiled!

John Milton (1608–1674)
English poet

104

Divine imaginings, like gods, come down to the groves of our Thessalies, and there

in the embrace of wild, dryad, reminiscences, beget the beings that astonish the world.

HERMAN MELVILLE (1819–1891)
AMERICAN WRITER

WE STOPPED AND STARED AS THEY PASSED ABOVE US . . . .

THEIR FACES WERE PERFECTLY CLEAR TO US . . . .

THEY SEEMED TO FLOAT PAST US.

S. Ralph Harlow
American professor

THE GUARDIAN ANGELS OF LIFE SOMETIMES FLY SO HIGH AS TO BE BEYOND OUR SIGHT,

BUT THEY ARE ALWAYS LOOKING DOWN UPON US.

Jean Paul Richter (1763–1825)
German writer

Above my desk . . .

In finely woven robes . . .

Hovers a patently angelic visitor.

JAMES MERRILL (B. 1926)
AMERICAN WRITER

There was a pause—just long enough

for an angel to pass, flying slowly.

RONALD FIRBANK (1886–1926)
ENGLISH WRITER

ANGELS CAN FLY BECAUSE THEY TAKE THEMSELVES LIGHTLY.

G. K. Chesterton (1874–1936)
English writer

OUTSIDE THE OPEN WINDOW

THE MORNING AIR

IS ALL AWASH WITH ANGELS.

Richard Wilbur (b. 1921)
American poet

THE IMMORTAL SPIRIT HATH NO BARS

TO CIRCUMSCRIBE ITS DWELLING PLACE;

MY SOUL HATH PASTURED WITH THE STARS

UPON THE MEADOW-LAND OF SPACE.

Frederick G. Scott (1861–1994)
Canadian poet

The green bushes bowed as though

they had been visited by archangels.

KATHERINE MANSFIELD (1888–1923)
NEW ZEALAND-BORN ENGLISH WRITER

The industrious angel is small and quick-moving.

His aura is composed of a rainbow of vibrating

color to complement the ever-changing stream of

humanity he interacts with.

KAREN BLESSEN
AMERICAN ARTIST

116

Cupid is naked and does not like artifices.

Sextus Propertius (c. 50–15 b.c.)
Roman poet

It was first whispered among the seraphim and cherubim, and then said aloud among the angels and archangels, that he didn't even look like an angel!

And they were quite correct. He didn't. His halo was permanently tarnished where he held on to it with one, hot, little, chubby hand when he ran, and he was always running. Furthermore, even when he stood very still, it never behaved as a halo should. It was always slipping down over his right eye . . . or over his left eye. . . .

CHARLES TAZEWELL (1900–1972)
AMERICAN WRITER

[The] concept of angels' wings is drawn from their ability to move instantaneously and with unlimited speed from place to place.

BILLY GRAHAM (B. 1918)
AMERICAN CLERIC

. . . TO HAVE FAITH IS TO HAVE WINGS.

J. M. Barrie (1860–1937)
Scottish playwright

Faith is an excitement and enthusiasm: it is a condition of

intellectual magnificence to which we must cling as to a treasure.

GEORGE SAND [AMANDINE AURORE-LUCILE DUPIN] (1804–1876)
FRENCH WRITER

. . . ANGELS BELONG TO A DIFFERENT SPECIES, ONE WITH A FINER VIBRATIONAL FREQUENCY

THAN HUMANS ARE USED TO. THEY ARE BEYOND GENDER, BUT CAN BE SEEN

AS MALE OR FEMALE, DEPENDING ON THE BEHOLDER. THERE ARE MANY DIFFERENT KINDS OF

ANGELS—SOME MIGHT APPEAR AS MULTIDIMENSIONAL SPHERES, AS SHAFTS, SPIRALS,

OR CONES OF LIGHT, RANGING IN SIZE FROM A DOT TO A GALAXY.

Kimberley Snow
American writer

It is through our many joy-filled windows of receptivity that angels dare to fly right into our hearts.

KAREN GOLDMAN
AMERICAN WRITER

WHAT IDEA IS MORE BEGUILING THAN THE

NOTION OF LIGHTSOME SPIRITS, FREE OF

TIME AND SPACE AND HUMAN WEAKNESS,

HOVERING BETWEEN US AND ALL HARM?

Nancy Gibbs
American writer

C h e R u b s

Cover art and p. 44: *Music-making Angel*, by Rosso Fiorentino. Uffizi, Florence, Italy; Scala/Art Resource, New York.

c R e a t U r e s   o f   l i g h t

p. 8: *The Swarm of Cherubs*, by Jean-Honore Fragonard. Louvre, Paris; Reunion des Musees Nationaux, Paris/Bridgeman Art Library, London and New York.

p. 11: *Cupidon*, 1891, by William-Adolphe Bouguereau. Roy Miles Gallery, 29 Bruton Street, London , W1/Bridgeman Art Library, London and New York.

p. 12: *Birth of Venus*, by Alexandre Cabanel. Musee d'Orsay, Paris; Giraudon/Art Resource, New York.

p. 15: *The Immaculate Conception*, by Jose Antolinez. Prado, Madrid; Bridgeman Art Library, London and New York.

p. 16: *The Virgin in Paradise*, from the frieze of musical angels in the Chapel of Isotta degli Atti, by Antoine Auguste Ernest Hébert. Musee Hébert, Paris; Giraudon/Art Resource, New York.

p. 19: Putto playing the trumpet, c. 1450, by Agostino di Duccio. Tempio Malatestiano, Rimini, Italy; Bridgeman Art Library, London and New York.

p. 20: *Danae*, by Giacinto Gemignani. Museo Civico, Pistoia, Italy; Scala/Art Resource, New York.

p. 23: Angel with trumpet holding ten commandments, by Franz Xaver Schmaedl. Church of the Augustinan Canons, Rottenbuch, Germany; Erich Lessing/Art Resource, New York.

p. 24: Three putti in clouds, by Francois Boucher. Agnew & Sons, London; Bridgeman Art Library, London and New York.

p. 27: Initial "A" formed by an architectural structure with Galeazzo Maria Sforza kneeling in prayer, choir book, 1477, artist unknown. Wallace Collection, London; Bridgeman Art Library, London and New York.

p. 28: *Child Angel Playing a Flute*, c. 1500, by Bernardino Luini (c. 1480–1532). Fitzwilliam Museum, University of Cambridge, England; Bridgeman Art Library, London and New York.

p. 31: Illustrations designed by Jacqueline Mair and Roger la Borde©, London.

p. 32: *Air*, by Jan the Elder Brueghel. Louvre, Paris; Erich Lessing/Art Resource, New York.

p. 35: *Annunciation to Saint Mary*, by Peter Paul Rubens. Kunsthistorisches Museum, Vienna, Austria; Erich Lessing/Art Resource, New York.

p. 36: *Allegory of Sculpture*, by Angelica Kauffmann. Cheltenham Art Gallery and Museums, Gloucestershire, England; Bridgeman Art Library, London and New York.

p. 39: *Seated Nymph with Flutes*, by the studio of Francois Boucher. Wallace Collection, London; Bridgeman Art Library, London and New York.

p. 40: Angeli, by Andrea del Sarto. ©The Picture Library, San Francisco.

p. 42–43: *La Primavera*, by Sandro Botticelli. Uffizi, Florence, Italy; Scala/Art Resource, New York.

p. 47: *Christ, St. John, An Angel and a Little Girl*, by Peter Paul Rubens and F. Snyders. Collection of the Earl of Pembroke, Wilton House; Bridgeman Art Library, London and New York.

p. 48: *Some Angels Came*, by Mahvash Mossaed. Courtesy of the artist.

c R e a t U r e s   o f   l o v e

p. 51: *Adoration of the Shepherds*, by Anton Raphael Mengs. Museo del Prado, Madrid; Scala/Art Resource, New York.

p. 52: *The Martyrdom of Saints Rufina and Seconda*, before 1625, by G.B. Crespi with Pier Francesco Mazzucchelli. Morazzone and Giulio Cesare Procaccini. Pinacoteca di Brera, Milan, Italy; Bridgeman Art Library, London and New York.

p. 55: Illustrations designed by Jacqueline Mair and Roger la Borde©, London.

p. 56: *The Triumph of Galatea*, by Raphael Sanzio. Palazzo della Farnesina, Rome; Scala/Art Resource, New York.

p. 59: *Camera degli Sposi*, detail from the ceiling of the Palazzo Ducale, by Andrea Mantegna. Palazzo Ducale, Mantua, Italy; Bridgeman Art Library, London and New York.

p. 60: *Aurora Ascending the Heavens*, by Julien de Parme. Prado, Madrid; Bridgeman Art Library, London and New York.

p. 63: *Trinity with Saint Ursula and Saint Margaret*, detail of painting, by Antonio Maria Viani (c. 1555–1629). Location unknown; Bridgeman Art Library, London and New York.

p. 64: Untitled painting, by Kelly Stribling Sutherland. Courtesy of the artist.

p. 67: *The Birth of Venus*, by William-Adolphe Bouguereau. Musee d'Orsay, Paris; Erich Lessing/Art Resource, New York.

p. 68: *Charity*, School of Fontainebleau. Louvre, Paris; Erich Lessing/Art Resource, New York.

p. 71: *Danae*, by Tiziano Titian. Museo Nazionale di Capodimonte, Naples, Italy; Scala/Art Resource, New York.

p. 72: *Virgin and Child with Saints: Music-making Angel*, by Giovanni Bellini. Saint Maria Gloriosa dei Frari, Venice, Italy; Cameraphoto/Art Resource, New York.

p. 75: *Cupid*, detail of painting, by Giulio Cesare Procaccini (1574–1625). National Gallery of Scotland, Edinburgh; Bridgeman Art Library, London and New York.

p. 76: Musical angels with harp and organ, by Agostino di Duccio. Tempio Malatestiano, Rimini, Italy; Scala/Art Resource, New York.

b e A c o n s   o f   h o P e

p. 79: *The Annunciation to the Shepherds*, detail of cherubim, by Nicolaes Pietersz Berchem. City of Bristol Museum and Art Gallery; Bridgeman Art Library, London and New York.

p. 80: *Soul and Heritage of the Hispanic Cherubs*, by Orlando L. Ramirez. Courtesy of the artist.

p. 83: *Madonna in Glory*, by Bernardino Campi. Pinacoteca, Cremona, Italy; Bridgeman Art Library, London and New York.

p. 84: *Assumption of the Virgin*, by Philippe de Champaigne. Musee des Beaux-Arts, Marseille, France; Giraudon/Art Resource, New York.

p. 87: *Madonna and Child with Four Cherubs*, by Bartholomaeus Bruyn. York City Art Gallery; Bridgeman Art Library, London and New York.

p. 88: *Sleeping Child*, by Nicolas Rene Jollain, Wallace Collection, London; Bridgeman Art Library, London and New York.

p. 91: Cupid, by E. Munier. ©The Picture Library, San Francisco.

p. 92: Untitled painting, by Kelly Stribling Sutherland. Courtesy of the artist.

p. 95: Illustrations designed by Jacqueline Mair and Roger la Borde©, London.

p. 96: Birth of the Virgin, by Domenico Ghirlandaio. Santa Maria Novella, Florence, Italy; Bridgeman Art Library, London and New York.

p. 99: *Huntington*, by Beverly Bigwood. Licensed by VAGA, New York, NY.

p. 100: *Allegory of Painting*, by Angelica Kauffmann. Cheltenham Art Gallery and Museums, Gloucestershire, England; Bridgeman Art Library, London and New York.

p. 102: Untitled pastel, by Kelly Stribling Sutherland. Courtesy of the artist.

l i g h t s o m e   s p i R i t s

p. 105: *Amorini*, by a follower of Francois Boucher. Wallace Collection, London; Bridgeman Art Library, London and New York.

p. 106: Cherubs entwined, ©The Picture Library, San Francisco.

p. 109: *Saint Michael and the Demon . . .*, by Agnolo Bronzino. The Chapel of Eleonora of Toledo, Palazzo Vecchio, Florence, Italy; Scala/Art Resource, New York.

p. 110: *Portrait of the Young Prince Maurice of Bohemia as Cupid*, by Gerrit van Honthorst. The Trustees of the Weston Park Foundation; Bridgeman Art Library, London and New York.

p. 113: *Angels Playing with a Bird in a Landscape*, by Hendrik Willem Schweickardt. Rafael Valls Gallery, London; Bridgeman Art Library, London and New York.

p. 114: *Cupid in a Landscape*, c. 1510, by Giovanni Antonio Bazzi Sodoma. Hermitage, St. Petersburg, Russia; Bridgeman Art Library, London and New York.

p. 117: *The World*, tarot card, by Antonio Cicognara. Accademia Carrara, Bergamo, Italy; Scala/Art Resource, New York.

p. 118: Putti going around a fountain, by Agostino di Duccio. Tempio Malatestiano, Rimini, Italy; Scala/Art Resource, New York.

p. 121: The Two Angels, detail from *The Sistine Madonna*, by Raphael Sanzio. Gemaeldegalerie, Staatliche Kunstsammlungen, Dresden; Erich Lessing/Art Resource, New York.

p. 122: *Madonna and Saints*, by Rosso Fiorentino. Uffizi, Florence, Italy; Scala/Art Resource, New York.

p. 125: Illustrations designed by Jacqueline Mair and Roger la Borde©, London.

p. 126: *Leda and the Swan*, by Leonardo da Vinci. Galleria Borghese, Rome, Italy; Scala/Art Resource, New York.